Paula Sunshine

You've Been Timber-Framed!

'Your Guide to Living In Harmony
with an Ancient Timber-Framed Home'

Barry Harber PR

Front & back cover photographs show the author

First published 2003
by Barry Harber PR
Hill's Farm, Bury Road, Lawshall
Suffolk IP29 4PJ
bpharber@aol.com

ISBN 0-9545952-0-3

British Library Cataloguing-in-Publication Data
A CIP catalogue record for this book is available from the British Library.

Printed in Great Britain by
The Lavenham Press Ltd,
Lavenham, Suffolk.

Contents

Acknowledgements

All Photography - Barry Harber PR & The Author.

Advice and suggestions gratefully received from
M.D.J Chesterman and D Nisbet-Smith.

This book is dedicated to my long suffering husband who introduced me to the
wonders of timber-framed buildings, much to his regret.

Introduction

I've been timber-framed! Friends often remark I should have this statement printed on my T-shirts or better still tattooed on my forehead.

Those who know me well will tell you my main topic of conversation most of the time is about timber-framed buildings, their care and repair.

In my experience timber-framed home owners are unique. They love their timbered homes no matter how important or insignificant they happen to be and I have yet to meet an owner not fascinated by investigating the history of their ancient building.

Most homeowners I have got to know over the years through my work with timber-framed buildings have been special people who really do care about the future health of their houses. And not just because they want to protect their financial investment. They understand they are merely caretakers of an ancient building with the responsibility of passing it on at some time in the future in as good and well preserved condition as possible.

Of course, there are those home owners who do not see their role quite as saintly as all that. They may desire to alter the structure significantly, to adapt the building to suit transient requirements, to destroy much historic fabric or carry out repairs using wholly unsuitable methods and materials that have the potential, given time, to damage the very fabric of the building they claim they adore.

And there are a few people I have met who are not even certain they enjoy living in their timber-framed home, frustrated by the seemingly endless stream of repair work. However, once they begin to understand how their timber-framed building functions, the task of maintaining it becomes far less daunting.

Well, whatever type of timber-framed home owner you happen to be, this publication has been written to assist you to make an informed purchase and live in harmony within your timber-framed building. If you have already lived for many years within a timber-framed home, but have little understanding of the fabric of your building or how to repair it correctly, you too will be enlightened by many of the revelations within the following pages.

There are several good books available today which explore the more technical aspects of timber-frame repair. This book is not written in an attempt to replicate them.

It is however, written by the owner of a timber-framed home for the benefit of others. Its simple, clear format, has been deliberately designed to ensure the reader can easily digest and understand the information within.

I very much hope you will enjoy getting to know your building better than anyone else.

Dream home

Scour the pages of any 'property for sale' publication and you may find at least one of the following words and phrases used to describe some of the timber-framed homes on offer: Charming, idyllic, delightful, fine, stunning, character-full, superb, a wealth of beams, heavily timbered, immaculate, pretty.

With the right photograph, taken at just the right angle, almost any home can be made to look all of these and more. A lick of paint, mowed lawn, strategically placed planters bulging

with chemically enhanced begonias and there you have your 'dream cottage', neatly packaged, awaiting your excited arrival. **Figures 2 & 3**.

As the proud owner of a 16th century timber-framed home, I wouldn't choose any other structure in which to live. They make wonderful homes jam packed with character and history oozing from beneath every layer of paint and plaster. They all hold tantalising secrets of past residents and old uses waiting to be rediscovered.

Figure 2 & 3 *Idyllic looking thatched cottages.*

Looked after correctly, a timber-framed building has the potential to survive for a thousand years or more. The very oldest and rarest in existence in Britain today date from around the 1300's and are generally well documented. Despite this, owners featured in a variety of lifestyle magazines still insist William the Conqueror stayed at their house en route to Hastings in 1066 or The Domesday Book was written in their very kitchen, next to the range cooker, of course.

In reality, the majority of surviving timber-framed buildings date from the 15th, 16th and 17th centuries, and remain a testament to the incredible knowledge and building skills of the carpenters who put them together. Many of the fine timber-framed buildings around today were once the well built homes of comfortably off yeoman, not the hedgerow sticks cottages of landless labourers as some might suggest. Those poorly built, usually one roomed hovels, have not survived.

Timber-framed buildings have the potential to last indefinitely, provided they are repaired and cared for correctly, using traditional, natural materials and nothing else.

Many of the attractive looking period homes we see on the market today may at first glance appear to have been beautifully maintained and smartly kept. However, one should never be fooled by outward appearances. Cosmetic decoration can often cover up a multitude of sins where period buildings are concerned, especially those of the timber-framed variety.

You may already have discovered your dream cottage and initially be tempted to put this publication firmly back on the shelf. However, the wise will continue reading, assured in the knowledge that everything within the following pages is written with the timber-framed homeowners best interests in mind. Much of what you are about to learn has the potential to save you thousands of pounds and a good deal of heartache. So if this alone doesn't encourage you to read on, you obviously have more money than sense.

Nightmare

Let us start where at least some of you will be today, taking a good look at the estate agents property details you have been enthusiastically sent. They all look so smart, don't they?

Initially, you may be concerned with features such as the number of rooms and their dimensions, fitted kitchens, central heating, the overall attractiveness of the building together with the 'location, location, location', which, although important, should not be your No.1. priority where a timber-framed property is concerned.

However, by the time you have read through these pages I hope all of these will be firmly at the lower end of your 'priority list' and other, far more crucial details will move closer to the top. You may adore the recently laid Chinese slate adorning the floors throughout your potential purchase. Once you realise the damaging effects imperviously laid flooring can have on the structure of an ancient home, you will soon feel differently.

When viewing a property, unpopular as it may be to say, the more immaculate it looks, the more cautious a potential purchaser should be. Newly painted, plastered or filla' repaired surfaces can often be a sign something has been covered up, patch repaired or disguised. It is far easier for a buyer to make an honest assessment of the true condition of a property that has had little attention or money spent on it over the years. Given the choice, I would prefer to purchase and repair a ramshackle wreck than a seemingly perfect palace any day. You know exactly what you are buying and can better assess how much time and money you will need to spend in the future.

Many owners of 'over-renovated' properties I have spoken to often expound about the appalling condition their home was in prior to its 'complete renovation'. In reality, many old buildings were probably in a far healthier condition prior to some, so called 'repair works' than they appear afterwards. For example, a crumbling lime washed lime plaster wall coating may not look very smart, but it is a good deal better for the 'breathability' of the walls of an old building than a neatly gypsum plastered, vinyl emulsion painted surface.

'Has recently undergone extensive restoration, renovation, modernisation'. This is a sentence increasingly used in property details for many historic houses and one which always disappoints me. This description should also make you cautiously curious.

Sadly, for many properties this can often mean, 'has recently been gutted, stripped bare to the frame, every attractive original feature destroyed or modernised, leaving little left of the buildings charm and character'. It will almost certainly also contain at least one hideous, wood worm damaged, sandblast restored, reclaimed timber, purporting to be the original bressummer over a badly 'restored' fireplace in an over-modernised, fully fitted kitchen.

Where money is not an issue, speedy renovation of a property frequently takes place. This really is a big mistake as much of what is uncovered or revealed during work is sometimes little understood at the time. **Figures 4 & 5**. Few photographs or drawings of the structure are taken as many owners are in too much of a hurry to complete their project to be bothered with such seemingly unimportant records. It is only later on, when it is all too late, the relevance of destroyed or much altered features is realised and owners begin to regret the haste with which work was completed.

'Loads-a-money' can be the very downfall of any period property, not only a timber-framed one. Owners who can afford to change a building to suit their current requirements very often do so without stopping to consider exactly what they are destroying and its historic significance. Major structural changes are sometimes thoughtlessly made.

Figure 4 *Features uncovered during restoration - beautiful carving.*

Figure 5 *Features uncovered during restoration - a diamond mullion window.*

Years later, the results of inappropriate repair methods will usually become apparent to a future owner who is left to suffer the consequences, together with the repair bill. With properties changing hands on average every five to seven years, this is a sobering thought if you are about to purchase that smart timber-framed house, recently 'extensively renovated'.

The old saying, 'what the eye can't see, the heart can't grieve over', just isn't true where timber-framed buildings are concerned. In a couple of years that fungal growth lurking behind the smart new kitchen may have eaten its way through the timber sole plate, leaving your heart and purse with a good deal of grieving to do. So remember, if property details mention any 'extensive renovation', be warned.

Best kept secret!

In my opinion, some surveyors really should know more than they currently do about the timber-framed buildings they are employed to examine on behalf of potential purchasers.

Several years ago, always keen to further my knowledge, I wrote to various surveying practices inquiring if I could perhaps work for them for a short period of time.

I felt sure some of them at least would appreciate unpaid assistance when carrying out a full structural survey on a timber-framed building, even if this meant my merely taking notes.

Only one surveyor replied to my letter asking to see me.

After quizzing me thoroughly about my intentions, to my surprise he confessed that, despite being regularly employed to undertake timber-framed building surveys, his personal knowledge of them was not terribly good. Even more shocking was his admission that in the seven years training in order to qualify as a surveyor, only a couple of days were spent covering the subject of timber-framed buildings.

Many surveyors today, even those whose knowledge of this type of structure is at best acceptable, are still continuing to recommend repair works, such as the insertion of a damp proof membrane, which could easily have dire consequences for these ancient buildings.

A survey I recently studied on behalf of a potential purchaser recommended the new owner lift the only healthy 'breathing' original brick floor in the whole house to relay it upon a plastic membrane, despite there being no sign of dampness in this area.

Many full structural surveys omit to mention cement render or concrete paths surrounding a property, both wholly undesirable features which can easily lead to premature deterioration of a timber-framed building together with considerable expense to remedy.

When carrying out a full structural survey most surveyors will cover themselves by stating they cannot comment on any part of the structure they cannot see. Well, although they might be forgiven for not possessing X-ray vision, they should not be forgiven for 'passing the buck'. Anyone experienced in working with ancient timber-framed buildings should be able to carry out a reasonably accurate assessment of a building and in many cases give a good indication of the likely condition of the frame. Paying anyone a large sum of money to tell you only the blindingly obvious really is a waste of their time and your money.

At the present time, in my opinion it would appear to be the best kept secret that although some prudent surveyors are attending further development courses in order to improve their knowledge of timber-framed buildings, many more need to vastly increase their understanding of this type of structure in order to provide property buyers with a full structural survey worth more than the paper it is printed upon.

Top tips for viewing

So for now, let us imagine you have found it. The one. Everything you have ever wanted. It has that atmosphere, warmth. You have to have it, no matter what. You want to put in an offer now, before anyone else snaps up this 'gem'.

But hold on a minute, you're in love remember. And what do people in love always do? Let their hearts rule their heads. They buy timber-framed houses without weighing up the true costs involved in the future repair and care of the building. They sometimes have no spare funds to carry out even urgent works to their property, let alone minor cosmetic ones. They often bite off much more than they can chew, in many cases falling rapidly out of love with each passing year.

If you are the sort of buyer who likes to renovate timber-framed buildings to make a quick profit, please don't!

They do not make particularly good financial investments purely because the traditional building skills and techniques required to repair them correctly are labour intensive, time consuming and therefore costly, unless that is, you are able to carry out the majority of the work yourself.

Other homeowners rush headlong into house restoration with little or no experience of working with timber-framed buildings. They do not understand the materials they uncover or how best to repair them. Most sane people wouldn't even consider restoring a valuable antique without prior experience or a good deal of tuition. It is hard to understand why many homeowners feel qualified to tackle the complicated repairs involved with an ancient timber-framed house, without at the very least going on a course or two.

So, with the old saying, 'forewarned is forearmed' in mind, let us now start to examine exactly what you should be looking at when considering buying a timber-framed building. You may think much of the following information would be covered in your surveyor's full structural survey. If you have an excellent surveyor, experienced with timber-framed properties, some of it may be. However, much of it may not, even though many of the points raised in this publication will help you better assess the true costs involved with the repair and care of your future purchase. If you are really serious about putting in an offer, first check out the answers to the following questions.

Pertinent questions to ask when buying a timber-framed building

1. What type of external **render** does the house have? Cement, lime or clay based? *Ref: page* 18

2. What **paths** abut the outside of the house? Concrete, stones, asphalt, bricks? What are the **external ground levels** like? *Ref: page* 24

3. What **internal plaster** does the property have? Lime plaster, gypsum plaster, plaster board? What type of **paint** has been used on external and internal wall surfaces? Lime wash, distemper, 20th century modern vinyl or oil based paints. *Ref: page* 26

4. Do **wattle & daub in-fill panels** still reside between stud work or have these been replaced? What with? *Ref: page* 29

5. Does the property have **brick in-fill** instead of more common wattle & daub? *Ref: page* 34

6. Is all of the **timber-frame visible**, particularly the sole plate and ground floor wall studs? *Ref: page* 36

7. Are any of the external walls obscured internally with **fitted furniture** such as wardrobes, cupboards or kitchen units? *Ref: page* 38

8. Has any of the **timber-frame** been **removed** in the past? If so, might this affect structural stability in the future? Check tie beams, collars & braces, corner or storey posts in particular. *Ref: page* 39

9. Are the timbers painted with an **impermeable (waterproof) coating**? Such as vinyl or oil based paint/stain/tar? *Ref: page* 42

10. Is there evidence of an inserted **DPC (Damp proof course or membrane)**? What type of flooring covers the ground floor? Concrete, bitumen, ceramic (glazed) tiles bedded in impermeable mortar? Where **ground floors** are of brick, are these dry laid on sand or chalk without a damp proof membrane, or cement laid on top of a damp proof membrane? *Ref: page* 46

11. Is there evidence of damage caused by **wood boring insects** - is this ancient or active? *Ref: page* 50

12. Have any of the **windows** been replaced with **uPVC double glazing**? If the property is Listed, did the replacement windows have Listed Building Consent? *Ref: page* 52

13. Has any brickwork i.e. chimney stacks or nogging (in-fill between stud work) been re-laid or **re-pointed** using cement mortar and not lime? Has any brickwork been **rendered** over with cement or gypsum based products? Especially check the base of ground floor walls, both within and without the property. *Ref: page* 55

14. Has any internal brickwork, especially flooring, been **'sealed'** with an impermeable coating such as sealant or varnish? *Ref: page* 57

15. Is the roof area well **ventilated**? What type of barrier (if any) exists between roofing materials and rafters? Has **spray foam insulation** been used beneath roofing fabric (tiles, slates or thatch) ? *Ref: page* 59

16. Have any 'modern' **extensions** been added? Do they have Listed Building Consent? *Ref: page* 64

17. Is the property **Listed** by English Heritage? *Ref: page 67*

18. Is the property **semi-detached or terraced**? Is it situated in a town or the countryside? *Ref: page* 70

19. Will it be used as a holiday home? *Ref: page 71*

In this book I will explain why the answers to these questions are so important. Why inappropriate materials which may have been used in the past have the potential to cost you, the new home owner, plenty of time and money to put right. How the very fabric of your ancient home should work best and why the two key words with regard to all timber-framed buildings are 'breathability' and 'flexibility'. Always keep both of these in mind when you, or those you employ are working on your home in the future and you will never go far wrong.

The good old days

Prior to the 20th century, although many timber-framed buildings remained in a poor state of repair, they were probably in much healthier condition than some of the smartest looking today. Before the increased use of modern building materials such as cement, gypsum plaster, various types of filler and modern, vinyl or oil based paints, the average flexible, incredibly well ventilated, breathing timber-frame would have suffered little of the structural deterioration regularly encountered today.

It is worth bearing in mind when examining decaying timbers within a timber-framed building, a great deal of this type of structural decay has almost certainly occurred in the last 100 years, much of it in the last fifty. In many cases this is generally through the use of inappropriate repair materials together with lack of air flow throughout a building.

Natural lime, chalk or clay based plasters, renders, washes and mortars were the main constituents originally used throughout all timber-framed buildings. The timber-frame skeleton was usually made from durable green oak, although other woods, such as elm, were also used, with the in-fill panels situated between the timber stud work usually being of wattle and daub construction. Where the timber-frame was covered over, lime or clay daub plastered walls and ceilings were supported on nailed wooden laths. Internally the daub panels in lower status homes may have originally been left without plaster and even without lime wash in some cases, their natural clay surface visible inside. The spaces between the timber ceiling joists of ground floor rooms throughout many homes would also originally have remained without plaster to begin with, the floor boards of the rooms above exposed to view. Plastering of any sort would have been a later luxury for many lower status homes and made living more comfortable, cleaner and convenient. Of course there are a dozen or more variations on this theme, not to mention regional differences. But the materials used throughout the country were basically very similar, even where construction methods differed.

Whilst lime, chalk, clay, oak, hazel and straw all provide breathability, flexibility and permeability, cement, gypsum and modern paints do the opposite, trapping moisture, encouraging the premature deterioration of the frame.

Timber-framed buildings were originally built on shallow foundations, sometimes of no more than a few courses of brick, or a few inches of stone or flint/chalk rubble. Although meagre, this base afforded adequate protection from moisture damage to the timber sole plate, sometimes referred to as the sill beam, resting above. Dampness would not have been a problem, therefore neither would fungal growth or beetle attack. This was mainly because of copious amounts of air flowing in through unglazed, or at the very least, terribly draughty, ill-fitting glazed mullion windows keeping moisture levels to a minimum.

It is therefore not surprising our ancient homes are feeling just a little bit suffocated these days. Many homeowners display a positive paranoia for sealing up draughts, fitting excessive insulation, hermetically sealing up their properties from top to toe. Even inorganic modern homes can show signs of fungal growth after prolonged periods without adequate ventilation.

The Here and Now

So, if we want to live a long, stress free, contented life within a beautiful, historic timber-framed home, what course of action is needed to rectify the points raised within our check list? And why should we even bother trying? The house looks fine, apart from a bit of damp here and there. Nothing a sealant and lick of paint wouldn't cover up nicely.

If only this were true. If you are someone who refuses to believe any of the advice written within these pages you could eventually, given time, find yourself saddled with a property nobody wants to buy. While you happily ignore the signs of frame rot, your building could be descending in value with each passing year, costing more and more for a future buyer to put right, if at all possible. And remember, a repair carried out correctly once, using appropriate materials, may seem expensive and time consuming, but will be a lot less hassle in the future than a bad repair using the wrong products carried out time and time again. **Figure 6**.

Figure 6 *A bad repair carried out time and time again.*

1. Render

Throughout the 20th century cement and gypsum based materials were increasingly used in the repair of timber-framed buildings. Sadly, those unaware today, continue to render and plaster using these products which, because of their impermeability and rigidity, are wholly unsuitable for use on a flexible timber-framed building. Hopefully, with more and more public awareness this will eventually become a rarer practice.

It is easy to imagine how the use of cement and gypsum became more and more popular.

By the early 1900's, building and repairing using lime was becoming unfashionable. Lime was more inconvenient to use than cement and gypsum, more hazardous to handle, slower to set and dependent on the right weather conditions for success. Knowledgeable tradesmen experienced in the application of lime-based products were literally dying out, their skills with them. Cement and gypsum must have seemed like 'wonder' products. They set quickly and were not affected by the weather which, unlike lime, meant buildings could be worked on both inside and out all year round. Nowadays, cement can be mixed using a mechanical mixer, unlike lime plaster/render and mortar which takes time and physical energy to produce. Cement and gypsum plaster are tough and hard. Lime, by comparison is softer and therefore wrongly considered weak and inferior.

No one a hundred or even fifty years ago realised the devastating effect marvellously convenient cement & gypsum would eventually have on the average timber-framed building.

Consequently, throughout the 20th century thousands of timber-framed buildings across Britain that had survived in pretty good condition for up to 500 years or more in some cases, were entombed in smart new cement render. **Figure 7**.

Figure 7 *1960's cement render on a 17th century timber-framed building.*

At first glance buildings must have looked wonderful, when compared with the scruffy, dilapidated and neglected lime rendered buildings they replaced. I have viewed many photographs of timber-framed properties taken in the late 19th and early 20th centuries, their original undulating lime render in an appaling state with huge patches missing. It would have been simple back then, and even today, to assume any lime based render was inferior and should be completely replaced with lovely, durable cement.

But, one should remember, the shabby lime render seen in old photographs, if not the original, would probably have been at least 100 years old. The properties' occupants, almost certainly tenants who did not possess the skills, money or incentive to repair homes they had no financial interest in. By the 1960's, landlords, hard up after two World Wars, long running tithe disputes together with various farming depressions, had little desire to spend money repairing and maintaining houses they would have preferred to demolish. It is not surprising these sad little hovels ended up in such a poor state of repair. Back then, if a timber-framed property wasn't incased in cement from top to toe, it was often pulled down to make way for a smart new bungalow. Many villages today, including my own, must mourn the demise of dozens of beautiful, historic buildings from their landscape, many of which had survived relatively unscathed since the 15th and 16th centuries. But there we must leave history in the past and move forward to the present.

Returning to the question of render, it never ceases to amaze me when I study a surveyor or estate agent's report on a timber-framed building and I read the words, 'the property has rendered and colour washed elevations'.

One does not need to be an expert (or a member of the RICS) to see a building is rendered. 'What is it rendered with?', has to be the pertinent question to ask. If your surveyor cannot tell you what material(s) the render and paint is made with, find one who can and one who realises the importance of this question.

A timber-framed building with cement render has the potential to cost thousands of pounds to repair in the future.

Of course, pressured to give you anything like a straight answer, most surveyors might say they couldn't possibly comment on the type of render, that is without first taking samples for scientific analysis.

Perhaps this has to be the future for timber-frame ownership. To omit such an important part of a full structural survey on the grounds of ignorance is simply unacceptable. After all, the external render is a major component of the full structure.

If by this point, you are still a little unclear about the seriousness of the problems caused by cement render, the following offers a brief and simple explanation.

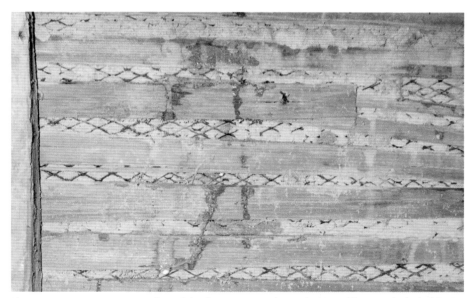

Figure 8 *Rain water penetrating through hairline cement render cracks (viewed from inside the building).*

Figure 9 *A concrete path and impermeable coatings trapping moisture beneath the sole plate.*

Cement render is extremely hard, inflexible and not as permeable as a render made with lime. Timber-framed buildings are quite the opposite, being flexible, expanding and contracting with the seasons. They require air flow, are able to accommodate slight movement in high winds and absorb moisture, allowing it to harmlessly evaporate back out again throughout the whole structure.

As our timber-framed building adjusts to seasonal changes, a hard, inflexible cement render will inevitably crack. No matter how tiny the crack, rain water will find its way into the wall through these openings, becoming trapped between timber-frame and external render. **Figure 8**. Although a lime rendered building may still allow a certain amount of water ingress, this can evaporate back out again through the structure, leaving timbers unaffected. Cement render traps moisture in, which in turn soaks into the timber-frame. This leaves wood vulnerable to fungal growth and/or insect attack. Most damage to a timber-framed building is aided by cement render and cement flooring which both tend to trap moisture around the base of a building, the sole plate area. **Figure 9**. Once render is removed, one often finds the sole plate (generally the outer half) and bottom foot or so of most of the stud work is in poor condition. Where water enters a building or becomes trapped higher up, stud work above ground floor level may also be affected, but as water tends to travel downward most decay is generally concentrated around the base of a timber-framed building. **Figures 10, 11 & 12**.

Figure 10 *Sole plate deterioration encouraged by cement render.*

Figure 11 *Water ingress causing cement render crack and...* **(See figure 12)**.

Figure 12 *rotting of jetty joist below.*

Decay of the timber-frame can be further accelerated by impervious render coatings and 'plastic' spray paint systems. Due to movement of the timber-frame and/or frost action, these coatings eventually crack , allowing water to enter, trapping it inside the wall. **Figure 13**.

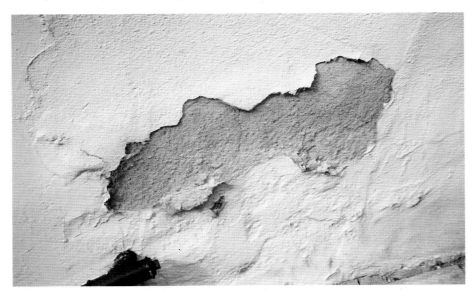

Figure 13 *Impermeable render coatings flaking due to trapped moisture beneath.*

Where drain or soil pipes are attached to a building through render, cracking will often occur here as well.

With all of this in mind, as one might imagine, the major cost of cement render replacement (with lime) is in the expensive repair of the timber-frame. When viewing a timber-framed property which has cement render externally and the timber-frame plastered over internally, beware! Parts of the frame may not exist anymore. At the very least, several timbers may possess little structural integrity and require extensive repair.

N.B. If you do decide to go to all the trouble of removing cement render, you will find it is almost certainly supported on metal mesh, which in many cases has rusted away over the past fifty years or so, leaving the cement bravely holding itself up. Metal mesh does have a degree of flexibility, but because its metal edges are reasonably sharp, these can sometimes cut off the render 'hooks' which protrude at the back of the mesh. Thousands of these little hooks will be relied upon in the future to hold on your new lime render, so think carefully about your choice of support. Sawn or split wooden laths are a much better choice.

When repairing lime render and using scaffolding, take great care. Make sure scaffolding companies employ the use of scaffold pole-end protectors. I have lost count of the number of render cracks I have seen caused by the unprotected ends of these poles wedged tightly into render. The same tip should also apply to window cleaners with their ladders.

2. Paths & External Ground Levels

Paths directly abutting a timber-framed building are an important consideration. **Figure 14**. Ground moisture harmlessly evaporates through materials such as earth/grass, gravel/stones, or bricks, tiles and stone slabs, all laid on sand, and/or directly upon earth.

Where paths are made from materials such as asphalt, concrete or even cemented-in tiles, stone slabs or bricks, moisture can become trapped. This can find its way along the ground and up through the walls of a timber-framed building. Moisture unable to easily evaporate can cause damage to both timber-frame and in-fill over time.

It is a simple and relatively inexpensive enough job to remove unsuitable paths surrounding a detached timber-framed

Figure 14 *Digging up concrete paths.*

building in a rural situation. However, if the building is in a town or village street, where impermeable paths or roads have been laid right up to the property walls, removal of these may not be easy, or even possible. This is especially so where the path is a public highway or pavement and does not legally belong to the property.

Figure 15 *A gravel breather strip between property and patio.*

Where dampness is detected around the base of the walls, it is highly likely an impermeable floor surface is a major contributor to the problem. When viewing a timber-framed property in this situation, speak with the local authority responsible for paths and roads (highways), to ascertain exactly where you would stand, should the removal of such a path be required in the future. In some situations it might be possible to create a simple gravel soak away gap, (not a French drain), between the building and the impermeable path to prevent moisture becoming trapped. **Figure 15**. However, care should be taken not to excavate below the plinth/foundation beneath the sole plate of a building, as this could lead to movement.

One of the many benefits of removing an impermeable path surrounding a timber-framed building is the discouraging effect this has on the ant population. These industrious and very clever insects appear to enjoy the cool, dark, damp conditions to be found beneath concrete paths or slabs. Unfortunately for the home owner this often means burrowing into the floors and walls of the house attached to the path, in the case of flying ants, frequently hatching out at the most inconvenient times. This usually takes place five minutes prior to the arrival of dinner guests you were hoping to impress. It is always a little difficult to expound the delights of timber-frame home ownership with little black insects dropping from the ceiling into ones crème brûlée. So dig up those impermeable surfaces and kill two birds with one stone.

Where external ground soil or man-made paths have risen above their original levels over the centuries, these should be carefully cleared away from the external walls of the property, taking care not to excavate below the buildings foundations.

3. Internal Plaster and Paint

Most home-buyers would be delighted to find a smartly decorated, neatly turned out property to view. However, for the very same reasons mentioned previously, it is important to investigate exactly what materials cover the internal walls.

You may love the three beautifully applied coats of Cinnamon Spice painted over the walls of the Tudor dining room, but if the plaster is gypsum and not lime and the paint is a modern, vinyl or oil based type and not lime wash or water-based distemper, the timber structure beneath these products could be in poor condition, unable to breathe. Once again any water ingress will become trapped, leaving the timber-frame vulnerable to fungal growth and the inevitable beetle attack.

There are several different combinations of traditional internal wall in-fill (the material between stud work) and finishes to consider. However, the two predominantly found throughout most timber-framed buildings are wattle and daub and lime plaster.

Wattle and daub is made with clay, straw and water (and cow dung historically, but this is not necessary), lime plaster is made with lime (putty) and crushed chalk mixed with copious amounts of animal hair which prevents shrinkage, cracking and holds the plaster together once dry. Several coats of lime wash, with or without a natural pigment (colour) are usually applied to finish. These products are natural, accommodate slight movement, are breathable and permeable. Unlike most modern products commonly on sale throughout many DIY stores, instead of trapping moisture, they allow it to evaporate and work in harmony with the timber-frame.

In the past, home owners often papered over these permeable surfaces, possibly because they did not understand their composition or how to repair them. Maybe they disliked the uneven surface or just thought they would look smarter covered. For whatever reason, papering over them did hide a multitude of sins, allowing owners to use modern vinyl or oil based paints which would not have easily adhered to the porous lime plaster surface.

All this, of course, has done nothing to improve breathability, trapping even more moisture throughout the home, especially in areas where plaster covers internal stud work.

For the same reason, modern paints should not be applied directly to lime plaster or lime-washed surfaces. In order to get modern paints to adhere to old lime or chalk based distemper washes, owners resort to applying an impermeable sealant first which serves only to trap moisture inside the panel. **Figure 16**.

Apart from being a healthier product for a timber-framed building, pigment coloured lime wash has a wonderful, uneven texture many admire, with a finish most modern paints find

Figure 16 *Removing impermeable paints from clay daub panels between rafters.*

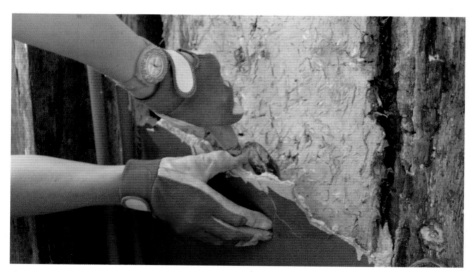

Figure 17 *Gypsum plaster and vinyl paint being removed from a wattle and daub panel.*

difficult to achieve. Although colour choice is limited to natural earth pigments, these are very much suited to ancient buildings.

I often see homeowners in the paint-mixing sections of DIY stores, walking around in a daze, spending hours trying to match the very same shade of their favourite tea towel, stressed out by the sheer magnitude of colour choice. It is only then I realise how fortunate I am, being limited to the relatively small selection of natural pigments!

When viewing a timber-framed property today, it is highly likely both internal and external surfaces will be painted with materials of the modern, less permeable variety, unless you are fortunate enough to find a house which has not been decorated for a hundred years, or has been wonderfully restored by a knowledgeable owner. Where impermeable surfaces exist, these should be carefully removed to allow the walls to breathe. If you are indeed fortunate, original lime plaster and/or daub may still lie beneath more recent plaster or paint and this can generally be repaired. **Figure 17**.

Ceilings throughout a timber-framed property should also be of lime, chalk and hair plaster construction. Although a change to gypsum ceiling plaster will not actually affect the health of a building in the same way as external walls would, apart from in a roof area where in-fill between rafters should be of a breathable type, gypsum plaster ceilings set far too hard and will not accommodate the sort of movement constantly experienced throughout a timber-framed building. Gypsum, unlike lime plaster, does not contain hair and is much more brittle. Applied to a flexible timber-frame, especially the ceiling, it will forever crack and require regular repair as people walk around upstairs.

If you are lucky enough to have lime plaster ceilings throughout your timber-framed property, do not even consider replacing them, no matter how dilapidated they may appear. Even the most horizontally challenged lime plaster ceilings can be repaired. By doing this you will save yourself time and money, at the same time protecting the fabric of your ancient building. This is something you may not begin to appreciate until work is finished and you begin to sit back and enjoy your beautifully restored home.

When compared with original lime plaster and daub in-fill, plaster board covered with gypsum plaster is quite unattractively flat and sits awkwardly with the irregularities of the timber-frame. If you are in any doubt about this, look closely next time you visit an over-renovated timber-framed building. They always seem to have lost something, a vital part of their history, far too hastily carted away in a skip.

Think carefully before you destroy an important part of your building. It is impossible, to replace original fabric once it has been removed. Estate agents' property details always rave about 'original features'. They will sell your home in the future, so look after them.

And don't forget, many high status timber-framed buildings originally displayed wall and sometimes ceiling decoration. This was often painted over at a later date. By removing original lime plaster, you could unwittingly be destroying something wonderful and unique. Hundreds of timber-framed homes have exposed timbers, very few ancient wall or ceiling decoration.

4. In-fill

Most people, whether they live in an ancient timber-framed house or not, delight in the undulations of wattle and daub, the materials used to fill in the gaps between the studs. **Figure 18**. The tactile surface always invites visitors to feel the lumps and bumps, often

caused by hazel rods or stones and chalk to be found beneath the hard clay crust. Once coated in lime (wash or plaster), the unique appearance of wattle & daub is enhanced even more, as lime and pigment distribute themselves unevenly across the surface, resulting in a textured look many interior designers endeavour to create today using a variety of paint techniques.

If you are a home owner who prefers flat walls and smooth, wipe-able surfaces, stop reading this instance. Flail yourself with the nearest hazel twig to hand and above all, don't buy a timber-framed building!

Immediately after purchase, which is often during the 'extensive renovation' of a property, many timber-framed buildings can lose their wattle and daub in-fill panels. **Figure 19**. For some strange reason many

Figure 18 *The delightful undulations of lime washed wattle and daub in-fill.*

Figure 19 *'Extensive renovation'.*

consider it an inferior building material. They have no idea what it's made from, how it's made, how it is repaired or how important it is to the stability and well being of a timber-framed building. Many home owners seem only to value the timber-frame itself.

This is nonsense when one considers wattle and daub in-fill accounts for at least 50% of the whole structure and a key element at that. Replacing wattle & daub and lime plaster in-fill four hundred years old or more in many cases with any modern equivalent, is akin to replacing the panels of a 16th century oak coffer with MDF.

Of course, much of this is not helped by the fact certain builders employed to 'renovate' timber-framed buildings have little idea of what they are looking at either. Ask your builder if they know what the original panels were made from and how they were put together. If they cannot tell you, you have the wrong person for a conservation repair job.

Wattle and daub is an ancient skill. It isn't surprising many in the building trade today do not understand how to repair it.

Having said that, it is a fairly simple craft to master and the materials inexpensive and widely available - clay, straw, hazel and natural string.

Fortunately, today there are increasingly many excellent traditional building skills courses available which aim to teach both homeowner and those in the building industry many of the techniques required to repair wattle and daub, lime plaster etc.

As the owner, or prospective owner of an historic home, it is your duty to learn at least some of these skills in order to understand your building. Even if you do not intend carrying out any of the work yourself, it will help you better assess the suitability of people who do so on your behalf.

So why should any of us go to all the trouble of preserving wattle and daub?

Historic - You will be preserving a part of your building that in some cases will be as old as the timber-frame. I have viewed many properties where smoke blackened wattle and daub panels still survive in perfect condition, 500 years after the open hall fire that created the carbon-encrusted velvety walls has extinguished. What more could one possibly ask of any in-fill panel? Has it not proven its durability ten times over?

Practicality - Wattle and daub in-fill can be made to fit as snugly against the timber-frame as any modern filler or plaster. In-fill panels (between stud work) are usually the same depth as the surrounding stud work, each one being about 3 to 4 inches deep. The hazel, or oak framework supporting the clay daub takes up the centre two inches of the panel, the thick clay and straw mixture is daubed either side of the wattle frame. The whole panel locks together as the clay dries. These are the oldest building materials and techniques known to man, tried and tested over thousands of years. **Figures 20, 21 & 22.**

Figure 20 *The wattle framework which supports daub in-fill.*

Figure 21 *Weaving wattles.*

Figure 22 *Daubing a panel on a new green oak building.*

Soundproofing - If your property is situated on a busy road, the sound insulating properties of three inches of solid clay is extremely effective.

Insulation - Although there has been little research carried out in this area to date, it is commonly considered by homeowners who take the time to repair and care for wattle and daub in-fill that it keeps a home cool in summer and warm throughout winter.

Moisture - As already discussed, whether your property is cement or lime rendered externally, the walls will inevitably develop cracks here and there over time, allowing moisture to enter. Wattle and daub in-fill panels between stud work act like a sponge, soaking up water ingress before it has a chance to damage timber. This moisture then harmlessly evaporates through the wattle and daub panel. It is an extremely simple process, but it works rather well, provided there is nothing to inhibit evaporation.

If these helpful panels are removed and replaced with modern impermeable products such as polystyrene, plasterboard, gypsum plaster and modern paints, moisture can become trapped. Eventually moisture levels will increase, causing terrible damage to structural timbers by encouraging fungal growth and insect attack, all of which often takes place without the homeowners' knowledge, particularly where timber-frame wall studs have been covered over both inside and out. The walls behind a fitted kitchen are particularly vulnerable.

Stability - Many homeowners who remove wattle and daub in-fill are unaware the stability these panels give the timber frame. Each individual wattle and daub panel is itself a small timber framework of commonly, hazel, tied, woven or nailed together. (There are regional variations and even variations within each region). In many cases, this is usually tightly wedged or sprung into a system of slots and holes within the timber-frame, locking the whole structure together. When repairing or replacing in-fill, it is important to study carefully anything removed, in order to replicate methods of construction peculiar to your part of the country.

Once in place, wattle framework is quite rigid. Strong enough to support the extremely heavy clay daub, but with a degree of flexibility, very much like the timber-frame. It is worth noting one 'person-sized' panel 6 ft in height, 16 inches wide and 4 inches in depth weighs approx.' 20 stone wet and approx.' 10 stone once dry.

After the clay daub surrounding the hazel has dried, a new panel of wattle and daub is more difficult to remove than one might imagine. Some homeowners testify to the easy removal of certain ancient panels. This is usually only where the surrounding timber-frame has moved away from the panel or the hazel framework built to support the daub has deteriorated. In my experience, both defects are usually caused by cement render allowing water into the wall, preventing it from evaporating.

One can only imagine how effective dozens of these stout panels must have been when first installed. In the averaged sized two-bay house, there would have been almost 100 individual panels wedged between stud work, providing excellent stability, especially in the event of high winds.

Figure 23 *Cement rendered wattle and daub panels damaged by trapped moisture and beetle attack.*

Figure 24 *Wattle and daub panels unaffected by fire.*

When examining in-fill panels that are currently in poor condition, it is understandable many homeowners assume these are about to fall out of the wall, doing untold damage to innocent passers by. **Figure 23**.

Like many timber-framed buildings, these panels have almost certainly suffered centuries of neglect and have usually been covered internally in layer upon layer of suffocating paint, plaster and even wallpaper.

So it would hardly seem fair to blame wattle and daub itself for any failure. Repaired and looked after correctly, these panels have the ability and stability to last for many more hundreds of years.

Fire resistant properties - Little research has been carried out to test daub panels for fire resistance. Many home owners believe them to be highly flammable. However, **Figure 24**. shows a photograph taken of one of several wattle and daub panels in a timber-framed property where the roof was completely destroyed by fire. The oak frame of the building has charred significantly, but remains structurally sound. Beneath the (removed) lime plastered surface, the wattle and daub in-fill panels remain intact. This would be an especially comforting feature in a thatched building where clay daub is the in-fill between rafters.

Aesthetics - I have purposely placed this reason for looking after your wattle and daub in-fill last as it really is the least important. 'The right look' is just the wonderful advantage of retaining and repairing wattle and daub. If you treasure it as much as you do the frame, it will look after the frame in return. **Figure 25**.

Figure 25 *The versatility of wattle and daub.*

5. Brick Nogging (In-fill)

It is not unusual today to see brick in-fill between the stud work of a timber-framed building that was originally designed to accommodate wattle and daub.

Where wattle and daub was the original in-fill this should be evident from the holes, slots or slits cut into the internal, hidden faces of the timber frame. These can only be seen once in-fill is removed. I have also seen wattles fixed 'invisibly'. This was achieved by nailing the horizontal members (ledgers which run from stud to stud), to the outside of the timber-frame. The upright hazel rods, which sit inside each panel, were then tied to them. These ledgers would have remained invisible once rendered over externally, but can easily be seen on removal of render.

This particular method of wattle fixing was quite inferior because on deterioration of the iron nails fixing the horizontal ledgers to the timber-frame, panels were liable to lose their stability. Horizontal ledgers in a panel fitted in this manner are also more vulnerable to water ingress and insect attack, being closer to outside elements, with only the render coating for protection. It is also quite difficult to repair or replace such panels (using traditional methods, of course), without first removing the external render, which is not always desired.

Figure 26 *Herringbone brick in-fill laid with lime mortar.*

Brick in-fill is heavier than wattle and daub, and does not assist evaporation of trapped moisture as readily. It is generally seen arranged in an attractive herringbone pattern, the downward thrust of which locks the bricks together. **Figure 26**. Provided brick in-fill is laid with lime mortar (not cement) and only ever coated, where necessary, with lime plaster, render or wash, it should not completely restrict movement of moisture through walls. Possibly one point worthy of noting is that brick nogging, unlike wattle and daub, is not fixed into the timber-frame and generally relies solely upon its weight to remain *in situ*. Therefore, in the author's opinion, it is not as structurally secure as wattle and daub.

Repairing the mortar joints both between and surrounding brick nogging using cement can cause premature deterioration of the timber-frame. The use of inappropriate repair materials can trap moisture and cause a build up of corrosive salts.

Lead flashing is occasionally fitted to the bottom of in-fill panels externally, particularly when a new sole plate is inserted. This is generally carried out in an attempt to protect parts of the timber frame from the damaging effects of rainfall, but can actually trap moisture between lead and timber, speeding up decay. External wattle and daub and lime rendered panels without lead flashing fitted, allows moisture to freely evaporate, as both panel and stud work are constantly exposed to air flow, able to dry out unimpeded.

6. The Timber-Frame - is it visible?

Early timber-framed buildings usually displayed stud work both inside and out.

Over the centuries, sometimes because of fashion or simply comfort, part or all of a timber-frame may have been rendered or plastered over.

Where moated houses and those in very wet areas are concerned, it is not unusual to find stud work at ground floor level has deteriorated beneath later render and plaster. This is especially true if the building has received cement render during the 20th century, as this can considerably speed up deterioration of the timber-frame. Where houses were built in very damp conditions, all ground floor framework may have been completely removed at some point in the not too distant past. This was often replaced with brick up to first floor level.

Where framework still resides beneath render, it is highly probable much of it at ground floor level will require extensive repair or complete replacement, once exposed. It may seem unreasonable to expect a surveyor to comment on the state of any part of a timber-frame they cannot actually see. However, with a good knowledge of timber-frame structure and plan form, an experienced enthusiast should be able to work out where each timber stud originally sat.

The simplest method, where possible, is to follow the wooden pegs along wall and sole plates. These are the pegs which hold the tenons (the timber ends) into mortises (holes) in most of the timbers around your home. Strictly speaking, stud work should sit directly below, above or beside these pegs, depending on what function the timber is performing. However, one should not always assume evidence of a peg is conclusive proof for the existence of a timber. Timbers can be carefully cut out, leaving the tenon still pegged into the mortice, giving one the impression a timber is still there beneath later plaster.

Simply tapping along a wall with one's knuckle can give an indication something more solid lies beneath plaster, as a change in sound could signify the presence of a stud. Whether it is an original timber is another matter entirely.

There are companies around today that can provide a 'thermal imaging' service. This is used to detect the presence of timbers beneath render or plaster. If you are in any doubt about the existence of hidden studwork, it might be worth employing a service such as this prior to purchase. However, the true condition of timbers is more difficult to assess.

Ideally, if you have any doubts about the loss or condition of the timber-frame, with the necessary permission from the current owner if the house is not yet your property, one should excavate a small hole or two in either external render or internal plaster at a level where timber damage is commonly located, usually within the first couple of feet of the ground. **Figure 27**.

Figure 27 *Cement rendered moisture damaged wattle & daub (viewed internally).*

This may sound extreme and an imposition on the current home owner. However, having listened to so many tales of woe from timber-framed home buyers who have experienced the near collapse of part of their homes due to decaying hidden timbers, I think this section is especially worthy of note.

In some cases, the only material holding up certain parts of the timber-frame is the 1960's cement render. Once removed, the result of 40 years of trapped moisture together with fungal or insect attack can become only too apparent.

If you are currently thinking how lovely the plastered walls will look once the house is yours and you have exposed hidden stud work, be prepared, it may not be there anymore.

It is worth mentioning at this point, all repairs to the timber-frame are best carried out using green oak and not old reclaimed material, for several important reasons.

To begin with green oak is less expensive to buy, easier to work with and will result in a more honest repair than one carried out using reclaimed timber in an attempt to fool the visitor or a future owner into believing it is original.

Bringing old seasoned timber from another building into your home also has the potential to transport wood boring insects. Larvae may still reside inside the wood where chemicals it may have been treated with cannot explore.

Buying ancient reclaimed timber encourages the trade in stolen materials and can promote the wanton destruction of buildings, not beyond repair, but whose individual parts are worth more once dismantled and sold off piece by piece.

Using old reclaimed timber for repairs to an ancient timber-framed building also confuses house historians, sometimes making it impossible for them to work out a properties original 'plan form' (shape) and therefore its age. This may not interest you initially, but will do later on when you have time to carry out research.

Finally, using green oak will encourage more people to learn the ancient carpentry skills required in order to repair our historic timber-framed buildings. Something that is crucial for the future of our heritage.

7. Fitted furniture

Fully fitted furniture is not ideal for a timber-framed building. The straight, neat lines of a modern fitted kitchen always sit awkwardly with the nooks and crannies to be found throughout a timber-framed home and getting any carpenter to build a wardrobe or cupboard to neatly fit around the lumps and bumps of a timber-framed wall is always a trial.

But the reason why fitted furniture is unsuitable for a timber-framed building is not purely one of practicality. It is for reasons of convenience and the good health of your building.

As I have stated previously, breathability is the key to a healthy timber-frame, especially around the base of the ground floor walls or sole plate area. Fitted kitchen base units attached to internal walls at ground floor level in particular prohibit air flow. Problems commonly arise around the sink, where hidden pipe work enters/exits the building behind fixed units. Water pipes can leak or develop condensation on their surfaces which in turn drips onto the sole plate or floor. Unnoticed, for years in some cases, this moisture can cause fungal growth and the rapid decay of the sole plate, all out of sight, out of mind. **Figure 28**.

Figure 28 *Damage behind the kitchen sink - out of sight, out of mind.*

Even where leaks are detected, homeowners who have just spent thousands of pounds on a new fitted kitchen are often reluctant to dismantle new units in order to allow moisture damaged framework and in-fill to dry out.

Free standing furniture, apart from being relatively inexpensive, affords the homeowner the convenience of being able to regularly check the condition of frame and in-fill and allows plenty of air flow between wall and furniture. Where repair work to walls or flooring is required, free standing furniture is also simple to remove and reinstate.

The very same principles should apply throughout a timber-framed building where fitted furniture is concerned. Wardrobes and cupboards fitted internally to walls that are themselves exposed to outside elements are all potential moisture traps. Furniture throughout a timber-framed building should be easily removable and preferably free standing.

Tiling on the inside of walls exposed to outside elements, usually seen in kitchens, bathrooms and showers, is also ill-advised for all of the same reasons mentioned above. It is impossible to keep an eye on a frame you cannot see.

8. What parts of the frame are missing?

A common act of vandalism which can have a catastrophic affect on the stability of a timber-framed building is the removal of timbers by those ignorant of their structural importance. **Figures 29 & 30**.

Figure 29 *This roof collar was thoughtlessly cut to accommodate a new bedroom.*

Figure 30 *An iron bracket struggles to support the bridging beam above, which should rest on the jowl of the storey post to the right, now cut out.*

Certain owners set about hacking away at collars, tie beams, wall/sole plates, braces, storey posts etc., oblivious of their vital function to the building. Never mind about the roof spreading, pushing the walls outward, just as long as they don't hit their head on that blasted tie beam ever again!

Interestingly, I have read many full structural surveys where missing, structurally important timbers have not been given a glance, let alone mentioned in the surveyors report. Not one word within a 30 page survey mentioned all but one of the five original roof collars in a timber-framed house had been cut out, two within the last ten years. Perhaps this was because the current homeowner had both removed the timbers and commissioned the survey.

A full structural survey should mention the whole structure. Make sure yours does. When viewing, look out for any timbers that appear to have been cut. This is where those of you who have done your homework and understand the structure will benefit.

You should at least be able to see those timbers vital to the future performance of the building. We are not talking about ordinary stud work which is often, if undesirably, removed without too much structural deflection taking place. The timbers to be aware of are those which, once removed, might lead to extreme movement of the building or possibly eventual collapse of all or part of it.

One only has to walk along the main street of any historic 'picture postcard' village or town to experience the consequences of ignorant alteration of some of the timber-framed buildings.

Most visitors and tourists to such towns probably imagine all timber-framed buildings began life 500 years ago looking as wobbly and structurally unsound as they do today. That these ancient homes will ultimately end their days slipping slowly down hill, ending in a big 'jackstraws' heap at the bottom, unable to support themselves any longer despite the tender loving care of dozens of well meaning owners over the centuries.

In fact, it is all too often because of the intervention of past homeowners or those they employ who have little knowledge of timber-framed construction, that these beautiful, once structurally sound buildings have started to show signs of movement. **Figure 31 & 32**.

Figure 31 *Interesting!*   **Figure 32** *Very interesting!*

The majority of early timber-framed buildings were so over-engineered when first built they can often withstand the removal of many secondary timbers over time. By secondary, I mean timbers such as common stud work and not those which provide major structural support to the rest of the frame, such as tie beams and storey posts, to name but two. Having said this, I would not advise the removal of any historically important timbers, original or later inserted, where at all possible. Compromise your designs, not your building.

One of the most common timbers to have been cut through over the years is the tie beam which runs across the building from wall plate to wall plate. Where an upper floor has been inserted or the homeowner wishes to move upstairs from one end of the house to the other without the necessity for two separate staircases, part or sometimes all of this awkwardly situated, low level timber was often cut out to accommodate a new doorway. Provided other ties exist throughout the building, or an equally structurally supporting alternative tying arrangement has been put in place, an alteration such as this may not prove a problem. However, cutting through the tie beams of a timber-framed building, for whatever reason, is always ill-advised and could lead to movement such as spreading of the outer walls.

If the timber-framed building you are considering buying has a definite lean on one side or another, look inside the property to see if part of the frame has been removed.

You may find the alteration and subsequent movement occurred a hundred years ago or more and may not be anything to worry about today. Where possible, investigate when such an alteration took place. It may not be as long ago as you would like to believe.

Where pipe work for plumbing or electrical wiring is concerned many home owners resort to drilling through timbers or destroying old in-fill in order to conceal every inch of its existence. **Figure 33**. This is quite unrealistic in my opinion. In an ancient home, one must accept that most of the time modern day services should only ever be either cleverly disguised or displayed proudly for all to see.

Who really cares if a bit of pipe is exposed anyway? If you are really irritated by this sort of thing you could always do what a friend of mine does, polish the copper water pipes to within an inch of their life and display them proudly for all to see. Looks great!

Figure 33 *This wire could more easily have been positioned between wall stud and in-fill.*

Whatever you decide to do with pipes and wires, do not cut or drill through ceiling or floor joists in order to transport them discretely from one room to another. Unless that is, you have a burning desire to fall through the floor in the not too distant future.

Never forget, you are just one in a long line of people privileged enough to live in your historic home. If everyone chopped out 'just that little bit more', there would not be much left of the original building to admire.

9. Black Timbers

Why were timbers stained or painted black? This has to be one of the most common questions I encounter in my travels around the country working with timber-framed homes.

One has to make an educated guess based on the evidence available. And where timber-framed buildings are concerned there is always evidence, if we use our eyes.

When we reveal parts of a timber-frame we know for certain have always been hidden from view, we can discover how timbers appeared when our homes were first erected. There are usually several areas within a building which have remained sealed up over time, the most common one being the wall which closely abuts the side of a chimney stack. It is here, usually due to inaccessibility, the internal face of the timber-frame can remain unchanged for centuries.

Other areas to investigate are inside old fitted cupboards, generally the least altered areas in a building. I have discovered spere screens, jetties, ancient peg and plank shelving and even original lime wash pigment, all within the under-the-stairs cupboard. It is often the smallest and seemingly least significant rooms of a house that hold the greatest surprises and best kept secrets.

Whether timbers were left their natural colour or painted has a lot to do with the status of a house and its former occupants, what the building was used for and of course, fashion. In my experience most middle class yeoman farmhouses appear to have originally displayed internal stud work of natural wood. Some buildings may have been painted with white lime wash or even ruddle (red ochre). Higher status properties might well have displayed decorated stud work with hand painted patterns using several pigments, but this was generally the preserve of the wealthy.

In lower status homes even the wattle and daub in-fill may have been left its natural clay colour initially. Perhaps lime plaster and even lime wash were the preserve of the more affluent to begin with. Eventually most timber-framed buildings would have received smart lime plastering in the following centuries.

So when did our homes receive their zebra-like makeover?

Well, I like to blame the 'uptight, everything has to be perfect' Victorians. Although one must not forget, many homes that began life 500 or 600 years ago as 'hall houses' would have displayed smoke blackened timbers centuries after the open hearth had been entombed within the walls of a smart new chimney stack.

So it may have been this that prompted the later application of layers of black stain and paint we so often see today. What else does one do with an already blackened timber, but paint it even blacker!

The twisting and shrinking of oak as it dries during the first few years after felling and sawing produces many splits, commonly referred to as shakes. Some of these can appear quite drastic to visitors not familiar with timber-framed buildings. However, they should be reassured to hear this occurred hundreds of years ago and in many instances is usually of little structural consequence today.

In the past, lime plaster or clay and straw daub could be used to fill in these gaps. When painted over this produces a look of perfection as good as the day the timbers were felled, hiding a multitude of sins. Of course, once coatings are stripped from timbers, all imperfections are revealed in their glory. This is worth bearing in mind if you intend restoring your timbers to their original, natural colour. These attractive 'blemishes' give wood its much admired character.

Even today some owners continue to lovingly repaint or stain their timbers black in the belief this look is best suited to a timber-framed building. However, 'the look' should not be the homeowners first consideration. For a timber-framed building to function correctly, that is to breathe, to expand and contract with the seasons, to absorb moisture and release it back out again, timbers should always be left in their natural, unpainted, unstained, unwaxed, unoiled state.

Painting the timbers of your home with anything other than lime wash or water based distemper could potentially trap moisture, encouraging fungal growth and beetle attack. Timbers most vulnerable will be those of the outer walls and roof where rain water may seep in through tiny cracks. It is imperative any coating painted on the surface of the timber-frame is one that will allow evaporation of any moisture finding its way into the building. Even beeswax could inhibit this process and could therefore encourage moisture retention in timbers whose outer faces are in contact with external render, tiles or thatch. This is even more important where a property has cement based external render, as moisture can then only evaporate through the interior and not the exterior wall surface as well.

If the timbers of the house you are buying have been stained or painted black, ideally this should be carefully removed to allow the wood to breathe.

Figure 34 *The results of timbers carefully cleaned using a poultice.*

However, only methods which are non-abrasive, for reasons of conservation of historic fabric, should be employed to remove undesirable coatings of any sort.

There are various methods of timber cleaning on the market today and personally, I prefer the poultice type as these appear to cause the least damage to both timbers and surrounding in-fill. **Figure 34**.

Figure 35 *Apotropaic or ritual marks on stud work (Hexafoil or Daisy wheel).*

Blasting, using sand, grit, water or anything else, particularly in the wrong hands, can cause irreparable damage to timbers, removing much historical evidence such as apotropaic symbols (witches marks), carpenters (assembly) marks and taper burns. **Figure 35**. It can also destroy the very edges of lime plastered wall and ceiling in-fill panels, costly and time consuming to repair. A tell-tale sign of 'blast cleaning' apart from the dry honeycombed look of the timber-frame, is filler or wooden beading fitted around the edges of each in-fill panel in an attempt to disguise these gaps. **Figure 36**. In the case of Listed Buildings this method of timber-cleaning is usually frowned upon.

Figure 36 *The results of timbers hurridly cleaned using sandblasting.*

Home owners often choose blast cleaning because it can be carried out in a very short period of time and is therefore relatively inexpensive. It can be very messy, requiring the removal of all furniture prior to work. Blast in haste, repent for years to come.

Cleaning timbers by hand using a non-abrasive method, although time consuming, will help you understand the structure of your home. You will get to know every peg and timber and discover things about the building you might otherwise miss completely. All of which will help you assess the age and historical development of your building. Take time and reap the rewards.

10. Damp Proofing methods – Chemical Injection & Plastic Membrane

Timber-framed buildings were originally built with very little foundation. A few courses of brick, flint rubble or stone were laid with lime mortar directly upon the earth supporting the timber sole plate which runs around the base of a timber-framed building, affording it just enough protection from ground moisture. **Figure 37**.

Figure 37 *A flint plinth beneath a sole plate.*

Many ancient timber-framed homes still display their original sill beam, some in excellent condition considering their great age.

Sadly the same cannot be said for the many timber-framed homes that have fallen victim in the 20th century to the demands of certain building societies or ill advised home owners, many of whom have inserted damp proof courses or impermeable floor membranes where none should ever exist. **Figure 38**.

Figure 38 *An inserted damp proof membrane (beneath carpet) is pushing moisture towards the base of this interior wall.*

Some surveyors mistakenly diagnose rising damp when examining the ground floor rooms of timber-framed buildings.

This can often lead to unsuitable treatment such as the employment of damp proof injection around the base of walls or the insertion of an impermeable membrane (usually in the form of a plastic sheet) beneath finished flooring, neither of which will cure dampness, only make matters worse.

Walk along any street today where historic buildings remain, whether timber-framed or brick built, and one will often notice unattractive lines of holes which have been drilled into the base of property walls by damp proof injection companies. **Figure 39**.

This is carried out in a vain attempt to produce a damp proof course within the walls in order to prevent moisture from rising up.

Figure 39 *Drilling damage caused by damp proof injection.*

In my experience, damp course injection will do very little as it is practically impossible to ensure the chemicals used have penetrated through the wall and have not, as is usually the case, left gaps where moisture can creep through. The very action of drilling can cause lime mortar, render and plaster to break apart, brickwork to prematurely deteriorate and future buyers of your home to remark at the appaling state of the very foundation of the building, not to mention the cost of repairing such damage.

If a building is suffering from the effects of dampness or trapped moisture and fungal growth, try a few simple and inexpensive DIY solutions.

Ground floor dampness at the base of walls is commonly caused by one or more and sometimes a combination of all of the following;

- A solid impermeable internal floor (such as concrete).
- A solid impermeable external path around the house (such as concrete).
- A cement skirting or plinth placed around the base of the sole plate externally and/or internally.
- Hard, impermeable cement render together with impermeable modern (vinyl or oil based) paints used on wall surfaces internally and/or externally.
- Defective guttering or pipework.
- Lack of adequate ventilation.

To prevent dampness, together with its damaging relations fungal growth and insect attack, impermeable (i.e. non-breathing) internal ground floor surfaces such as a plastic membrane, concrete or bitumen, together with glazed tiles or cement laid sealed bricks should be carefully removed and replaced with floor surfaces that allow evaporation of ground floor moisture. Unsealed brick or unglazed terracotta pamments laid on sand or chalk directly onto the earth, without a membrane of any sort, would be ideal. **Figure 40**.

A timber floor could also be laid if preferred but would require an air gap between earth and flooring, with air vents around the edges. To accommodate a wooden flooring, some homeowners resort to excavating below foundation level to increase headroom in their low beamed cottages. This is not advisable and could cause structural movement.

Figure 40 *A new brick floor laid on sand directly upon the earth (without mortar).*

Originally, beaten earth would have been the internal floor surface throughout most timber-framed homes. As brick or pamments became more popular and affordable, houses were fitted with these making everything more comfortable and a lot cleaner.

Figure 41 *An old brick floor hidden beneath later tiling.*

Unglazed brick allows moisture to pass through unnoticed. In the past, occupants of our homes would not have encountered many of the damp problems we so often see today.

Everything would have been fine for hundreds of years until the advent of glazed floor tiles, linoleum and fitted carpets, which inhibit the evaporation of ground moisture. **Figure 41**.

I have visited many timber-framed buildings where dampness and fungal growth have been eradicated, practically over night, by the simple lifting of linolium or foam backed carpet and opening of a window or two, allowing air flow to work its magic.

If you are being persuaded to insert a damp proof course or impermeable membrane into your home, think carefully. I doubt very much whether your building actually needs one in the first place and unless the plastic membrane covering the floor continues through the walls to the outside, it is likely to do more harm than good.

11. Wood Boring Insects - Chemical Spray Treatment

My reason for including this section next is because a great many damp proof injection companies also have a handy little insect chemical spray division.

Most of the woodworm damage (flight holes) we witness around our timber-framed buildings today almost certainly occurred within the first few years of them being erected and is generally confined to the outer sapwood area of the timber.

Much of the sapwood was removed from timbers cut for higher status buildings, but it can often still be seen in timbers about many of our homes and is the part most vulnerable to beetle attack.

It is believed chamfering of the exposed edges of timbers (such as ceiling beams) was originally invented in an attempt to remove the more vulnerable sapwood area left at the corners of a square cut tree trunk.

Much of the time, moisture ingress, fungal growth, lack of ventilation and wood boring insects all go hand in hand, although wood boring insects do not necessarily rely on assistance from fungal attack in order to make the sapwood area of timber such as oak more palatable.

Excessive moisture will promote the growth of various types of fungi which quickly breed, using the timber as a food source, breaking it down.

Once fungi have begun to destroy the wood's cellular structure, even hardwood such as oak becomes more palatable to wood boring insects. **Figure 42**. Where conditions are favourable, beetle larvae can munch away contentedly deep inside timbers for several years before finally emerging and flying off as adult beetles. Spraying chemicals indiscriminately onto the surface of ancient, well-seasoned oak is therefore a futile exercise unless all of the other symptoms which may have lead to any infestation are also dealt with.

Figure 42 *Beetle flight holes in the sapwood part of an oak stud affected by rain water ingress.*

Where timbers are painted with impermeable coatings such as stain, paint, oil or wax, spray treatment is made even more pointless.

Deal with any moisture ingress such as the repair of render or guttering, increase air flow around the area and the fungi should die, being unable to survive in wood with a moisture content below about 22 %.*

The timbers throughout a well ventilated, heated timber-framed home should have a moisture content of less than 9%*, too low for most wood boring beetles to thrive, as these generally require moisture levels above about 12%.*

* See References and Bibliography section - Brian Rideout - Timber Decay in Buildings.

In many cases I have encountered, the cure for beetle and fungal attack is often a simple one. Not the difficult and expensive problem certain companies might have you believe.

12. Windows

Believe it or not, draughty windows and heavy curtains are the order of the day for a timber-framed building.

One has to remember this is how many of our ancient buildings existed quite happily for hundreds of years. Without window glass, very much 'open to the elements', ill fitting wooden shutters perhaps the only defence against driving wind, rain and snow. In other words, excessive amounts of airflow. **Figure 43**.

Figure 43 *Draughty, but healthy, unglazed diamond mullion windows.*

Even glazed mullion windows, a later 'home improvement' for many, would have been ill-fitting and draughty, leaking whenever it rained.

Many home owners who expose or reinstate mullion windows in their ancient homes soon realise why 'the window' evolved over the centuries, developing into the weather-tight examples we see nowadays.

Having said that, although we may find draught free, sealed unit, double-glazed 'eyes to the world' just the trick for our chilly bodies today, they are extremely unhealthy, even damaging to insert into an old timber-framed building for a number of reasons.

Firstly and most obviously they prevent air flow which, as we already know, is a must for the well-being of a timber-framed building.

A musty damp smell can sometimes greet the timber-framed homeowner on return from holiday where a building has been closed up for a prolonged period of time.

It is a little like leaving your sarnies in a plastic bag, sealed up tightly for a week. Imagine the mould growth you would encounter. Yet this is exactly what can happen, over a longer period of course, to an organic timber-framed house.

Do not forget, these buildings would have originally remained draughty all year round. Yet with each passing century we have sealed up our homes just that little bit more, increasingly causing problems with every passing decade.

It hardly seems appropriate to talk about uPVC windows in conjunction with an ancient timber-framed edifice. Fortunately, I do not know many timber-framed home owners who would even consider replacing their old windows with these.

Unplasticized polyvinyl chloride (uPVC) windows can destroy the character of any old house and their insertion usually necessitates the complete destruction of old windows many of which are easily repairable, historically interesting and often irreplaceable. **Figures 44 & 45**.

Figure 44 *An historic window well worth repairing (sliding sash).*

Figure 45 *An historic window well worth repairing (iron casement).*

Sealed unit double glazed windows, whether plastic framed or wooden, inserted into an old timber-framed building can cause a rise in humidity and mould growth due to a decrease in air flow. This can promote a feeling of cold and dampness, quite the opposite of what was intended.

It can cost more to repair an old window than to completely replace it with a bright, shiny new one and this is why some home owners are reluctant to pay out for repairs.

Anyone who cannot be bothered to maintain an old wooden window is obviously not going to be the right person to sensitively look after an ancient timber-framed building. So if this is how you feel, maybe a modern house would be more to your liking.

If you own a Listed timber-framed building, repair or replacement of any of the windows will require consultation with your local authority conservation officer and probably Listed Building Consent.

These rules and regulations are put in place in an attempt to try to prevent disastrous mistakes being made. Such as the homeowner I met who left a window company in his home to replace all the old windows with new. On his return he discovered they had cut out several of the delightful ovalo moulded mullions 'in the way' of the new, larger window, ignorant of their significance. To the window fitter, they were just a couple of old, manky timbers.

Always supervise work in your home, seek unbiased advice, obtain consent where appropriate, study the structure of your building prior to any work being carried out and never replace windows with new unless they are completely beyond repair.

Lastly, on the subject of windows, maintenance of them and the surrounding render is extremely important to the well being of the timber-frame. It is here rain water is most likely to enter the wall through render cracks which tend to develop outward from each corner of the window. A window left to rot will allow moisture into the wall and could end up costing you a lot more than the price of a new window.

13. Pointing

It is becoming rarer these days to find any pre-1900 building that has not been painstakingly, but incorrectly, re-pointed using inappropriate hard cementitious mortar.

I have viewed some magnificent Elizabethan brick chimney stacks that have sadly received far too much attention from DIY homeowners or builders only experienced in the use of cement. All of them believe 'they have the technology' to make brickwork look smarter and last another 1,000 years.

The sad truth is many of these stacks would have fared a good deal better had they remained completely untouched.

Because lime mortar work is a skill which takes time and patience to master, many who work on old buildings today prefer to use cement.

Cement based mortars set too hard for use with old, soft red bricks and externally exposed brickwork re-pointed with such unsuitable material will prematurely deteriorate. Moisture that would otherwise harmlessly evaporate through permeable lime mortar joints becomes trapped behind cement mortar. This build up of moisture can cause terrible damage to the outer face of soft red bricks due to a build up of salts and frost action during winter months.

One only has to walk around any historic town in Britain to view the damaging effect cement mortar can have on historic brickwork. Whilst the newer cement mortar in an old brick wall remains rigidly protruding, the surrounding softer brickwork can often be seen continually crumbling away, receding with each passing winter. **Figure 46**.

Lime mortar by comparison is relatively crumbly and very much more permeable, allowing water to evaporate through it leaving brickwork intact. It is the perfect partner for soft red

Figure 46 *Cement pointed, soft red brick.*

brick. Any historic mortar should always be professionally analysed and matched for repair on a 'like for like' basis.

Historic brickwork repaired using cement mortar not only looks ghastly but is damaging to the very fabric of your home. Unlike lime mortar, cement mortar is impossible to remove from the surface of a brick, which means old bricks can never again be re-used as many are today. The golden rule should be, do not re-point or re-lay old bricks with mortar which sets harder than the bricks or is impossible to remove from bricks once set. If you are in any doubt about the mortar your builder is using, get them to put a blob of it on a brick. Leave it to set. If you then have difficulty removing it from the brick, it isn't lime mortar as this should come off easily, leaving the brick clean.

For the very same reasons historic brickwork should never be rendered over externally using cement as this will inevitably crack allowing moisture behind. This moisture then becomes trapped between brick and render and after a few seasons of salt and frost action can lead to the deterioration of both. Internal brickwork, such as a central chimney stack should never be plastered over using gypsum plaster or modern paint, as the brickwork will absorb ground moisture at its base and this will become trapped, climbing ever higher in order to investigate an escape route.

14. Sealing brickwork

A question I am often asked is: 'what can I put on my internal brick surfaces to seal them to prevent brick dust continually falling?'

Homeowners often go to extraordinary and sometimes quite destructive lengths to expose brickwork and original timber surfaces only to discover they do not really like living with the inconvenience of what can sometimes be friable surfaces.

Many Tudor and Elizabethan brick chimney stacks were originally painted over internally with a deep red ochre pigment. This was called ruddle, reddle or ruddlin' to name a few of the many spellings used.

Once a brick stack was erected, the mortar between the bricks, whilst still wet, would have been carefully scored, both horizontally and vertically. The whole stack, including the scored lines, would then have been coated with a red ochre wash. Once everything was dry, the scored mortar lines, which can still be seen today in many cases, would have been carefully highlighted (painted) with a white, lime or chalk based paint. Alternatively, lines could be painted black, using charcoal.

Ruddlin' does not appear to have been carried out for practical reasons such as to prevent brick dust falling, but in order to give uneven bricks a uniformed and therefore higher status look. But perhaps it did 'kill two birds with one stone' and also helped stabilise the brick surface.

In houses of the more wealthy, brick built chimney stacks would sometimes receive a coat of lime plaster, completely disguising the brick surface. **Figure 47**. Whilst the plaster was still wet, this would have been scored to give the appearance of ashlar stonework, even higher status than brick. Of course, the very wealthy would have had the real thing, especially where stone was easily accessible.

Homeowners today prefer to see the brickwork of their internal chimney stacks, often going to great lengths to enthusiastically remove historic lime plaster and lime wash that in

Figure 47 *A beautiful early 17th century lime plastered, brick fire place, designed to look like stone.*

many cases was original. In some timber-framed buildings the area above the chimney bressummer may well have once displayed wall painting or decoration of some sort, so great care should be taken to avoid destruction of these when removing plaster. **Figure 48**.

Figure 48 *The removal of plaster above this bressummer revealed 17th century jottings placed on top of an even earlier wall painting.*

In an effort to clean up brickwork, abrasive methods are sometimes employed. Sand/grit blasting, wire drilling or scraping with metal tools removes the more durable and harder fired surface of the brick. Once this is done brick dust will continually fall, often becoming a constant irritation.

Although sealing historic brick surfaces with a transparent coating does stabilise the surface for a time, it can also trap moisture which rises up from the base of the wall/stack (in historic brickwork without a damp proof course) that would otherwise harmlessly evaporate through unsealed brickwork.

Sealant can look terribly unattractive on any natural surface, especially brick. It will ultimately fail at some point as determined trapped moisture inevitably pushes its way out. One will often see the sealant itself has started to deteriorate, flaking off, encouraged by the build up of moisture and salts beneath.

Outside the home many owners prefer to paint black the brick plinth often seen around the base of the walls of a building, believing this will protect bricks from moisture damage. Nothing could be further from the truth. Exposed brickwork is far healthier for a building.

Any paint that is not water permeable will only serve to increase moisture levels within the wall. Before too long the paint will flake off in an attempt to assist the evaporation process.

Where sealant or paint is tough enough to withstand and withhold moisture trapped in brickwork, over time the brick itself will begin to deteriorate and this could potentially lead to serious structural problems in certain circumstances.

With the necessary consent from your local authority, lime wash could be used to stabilise a brick surface and this would still allow moisture evaporation to take place. Brickwork should never be painted with impermeable paints, sealants or bituminous substances.

Note: Not all chimney stacks were originally of brick construction. Many early stacks were of the timber-frame and wattle and daub variety. Very few of these survive today as most have been replaced with more durable (less flammable) brick stacks.

15. Roofs - Ventilation

Whether your home has habitable rooms in the roof or not, it is vitally important this area is well ventilated throughout the year.

In the past, tiled roofs were often 'insulated' or more accurately 'draught proofed' using a variety of natural materials such as hay, straw or a lime mix sandwiched between tiles, referred to as torching. Because these methods were in no way perfect, they still allowed a fair amount of air flow around the building.

Whether a roof is thatched or tiled , any modern, inorganic membrane placed beneath roofing materials will inhibit airflow and unlike ancient or more natural materials, has the potential to cause a build up of moisture.

Of course, the healthiest roofs are uninhabited, draughty and full of spiders and cobwebs, handy for catching all those wood boring insects.

However, it is not unreasonable for homeowners to want to make the most of their properties and the roof void can offer great possibilities for additional rooms. But this is where we also have to remember our number one priority, breathability!

The roof area within a timber-framed building is sometimes converted giving little consideration to the effects of reduced airflow together with increased moisture levels. Original rafters within an unconverted roof space of a timber-framed building are often in fairly good condition, testament to the preserving effects of excessive ventilation.

On conversion, a roof area can become 'entombed' in a multitude of modern 'high tech' unbreathing products such as polystyrene insulation, plasterboard, gypsum plaster and modern paints, to name a few. These products are used to fill the spaces between exposed rafters, although sometimes they are used to completely cover over the whole roof structure internally where rafters are deemed unsuitable for exposure.

To add insult to injury a double glazed window, or two, might also be added in order to prevent any hint of air flow ever entering this 'shrine to suffocation'. This window is hardly ever opened as it is situated at the top of the house, possibly in an infrequently used room, out of sight, out of mind.

Hey presto! You have all the right ingredients for moisture build up, mould growth and the potential premature deterioration of the whole roof structure over time.

In an attempt to disguise the musty smell of decaying fabric, sweet smelling plug-in aroma diffusers are sometimes liberally employed, particularly prior to an inspection by a potential purchaser.

On moving-in day at my current home, I discovered no less than eight of these, one in every room of the house. A few days after I had 'binned' the lot an unpleasant smell began to permeate the whole house and I soon realised why the previous owner had invested so much money in the horrid things.

Throughout the 20th century, when a roof was re-thatched or re-tiled, impervious bituminous roofing felt or a plastic membrane was sometimes placed between roofing materials (thatch or tiles) and rafters. Both of these materials reduce air flow and prohibit evaporation of moisture throughout the roof space.

Today, so called 'breathing' vapour barriers are commonly used. These are believed to reduce the risk of water penetration, still allowing movement of water vapour throughout the building. In my opinion, even some modern 'vapour barriers' have the potential to significantly reduce moisture evaporation where alternative ventilation is not provided or the vapour barrier has been incorrectly installed.

Moisture must be able to pass 'through' the structure. Should rainwater find its way into roofing materials, it must be able to freely evaporate, not remain trapped between rafter and roof covering.

On the other hand, or other side, any build up of moisture on the underside of the roof, such as vapour caused by cooking, washing, bathing, living, etc., must also be able to pass harmlessly upward and outward through roofing materials.

If the moisture path is inhibited, water vapour can condense into water droplets on the underside of the cold, vapour barrier placed on top of the rafters between tiles or thatch. This can run down the underside of the barrier collecting at rafter feet which then become more susceptible to fungal decay and insect attack.

Where homeowners really do need to extend the living area into the roof, careful consideration should be given, not only to the method of conversion, but also to the materials to be used, to prevent reduction of air movement within this space.

When our timber-framed homes were first built, some of them would have been of the 'open hall' variety, that is open (in part at least) from ground floor to roof ridge. Perhaps the upper floor, where one existed, would have been used for storage only and not living or sleeping. As time past, occupants began to move upstairs, to make these areas more habitable.

Even where homes had upstairs rooms from the beginning, it is highly likely many of the rooms we use as upstairs bedrooms today, were once open to the roof, without a ceiling. This was especially so where lower status homes were concerned. Upper floor bedrooms, without log fires, must have been very uncomfortable during the winter months.

Throughout many thatched buildings today it is not unusual to see, provided this has not been removed, clay daub mixed with straw (the same mix used in the application of wattle and daub) plastered between rafters, directly onto the underside of the thatch. The thatch battens where often used to hold (key) the daub in place.

Although a later 'home improvement' for many of our timber-framed homes, this type of rafter in-fill is an excellent sound and draft proofing material, provided it has not been coated with gypsum plaster or impermeable paints. **See Figures 16 & 17** (page 27). When coated with lime wash, daub between rafters allows moisture to pass through unhindered. If plastered over and painted with non-breathing products, moisture can become trapped between daub and gypsum, encouraging the build up of mould growth, promoting a musty aroma around the whole building.

In roofs where rafters are not particularly straight, daub in-fill easily follows the undulations of timbers, unlike plasterboard which can be difficult to fit around awkward shapes. Daub can also accommodate the slight movement roofs are frequently subject to in high winds and provides adequate insulation, generally being at least two or three inches in depth when used as rafter in-fill.

One of the oldest building materials and methods of construction, it is not surprising wattle and daub is still one of the best today, especially for the environment.

Home owners not keen to use this method of in-filling, but still wanting a 'breathing' roof insulated with natural, environmentally friendly materials, could insulate between rafters internally using sheep's wool - increasingly available today in handy pressed together batts in varying widths and thicknesses. The gaps between rafters could then be battened across internally and lime plastered to finished. This would insulate, but not suffocate.

Where rafter depth is too shallow to allow exposure of rafters inside the roof, sheep's wool insulation could still be placed between rafters, but the whole roof internally would then have to be battened over and lime plastered, covering rafters completely.

There is a current trend to spray foam insulation under roofing fabric in order to secure loose tiles or slates and draft proof the roof space. Don't! As we have already discussed, anything which significantly reduces air flow around the roof void will be detrimental to the structure. Most foam sprays make reuse of tiles or slates virtually impossible. If you are considering purchasing a property on which this treatment has been carried out, you may wish to negotiate a price reduction to allow for re-tiling of the roof.

Missing tiles, slates or thatch will all allow water ingress. A repair carried out as soon as possible will prevent further, more expensive work having to be undertaken in the future.

Defective guttering is a very common sight. Often blocked with debris and growing plants, or broken and with pieces missing, guttering and down pipes can be one of the most

Figure 49 *Guttering or hanging basket?*

Figure 50 *Blocked neighbouring guttering causing decay of the timber-framed building to the right.*

Figure 51 *Drain pipe or planter?*

neglected parts of a building. Perhaps because it is considered by many an insignificant, almost invisible part of the structure, little thought is given to maintenance of what are important rain water transportation goods. **Figures 49 & 50**.

Blocked, leaking or overflowing guttering has the potential to cause considerable damage to any building, not to mention expensive repair work to building fabric damaged by water ingress and fungal growth.

In towns and villages where houses are adjoined, it is not uncommon for the down pipe on one property, perhaps yours, to carry rainwater from neighbouring gutters. It is therefore vitally important to ensure this pipe is able to cope during heavy rainfall. **Figure 51**.

16. Extensions

Even before the ink on the exchange document is dry, let alone the completion certificate, many homeowners begin to dream about extending their ancient home. No matter how large a building, to some it never seems quite big enough. Perhaps it's got something to do with a, 'my erection is bigger than yours' type of mentality!

Homeowners often view their property as a blank canvas, something to impart their taste or their own personality upon. This is usually done at the expense and very often loss of the personality or rather character of the old house.

Many ancient and idyllic cottages have been ruined by inappropriate extensions often doubling or even trebling the size of the original structure.

Of course, much of this work is positively encouraged by some architects, many of whom consider it their life's work to stamp their own personality and creativity upon the existing structure no matter how historically precious a building happens to be.

I have viewed several 'architect designed' extensions to ancient houses, many of which have necessitated the destruction of much original fabric in order to adjoin them to a building. Certain architects show little respect for the existing structure when designing an addition, cutting through original roof and wall timbers in order to accommodate their ideas.

"Houses must evolve", architects often state in their defence and perhaps this is true. But throughout the 17th, 18th and even 19th centuries extensions to timber-framed buildings were usually carried out using traditional materials and in a sympathetic style, one which sat comfortably with the original structure. It is precisely because these additions blend in so very well it is often difficult to detect which part is original and which has been added later.

Today, the wholly inappropriate 1960's flat roof extension or 'new millennium' all glass addition can be a real give away. In an attempt to avoid replicating any part of the original building some architects end up creating a bit of a monster which often bears no relationship at all to the existing house.

Many home owners remain in awe of their architect, afraid to express their own opinions for fear of offending. Don't be bullied. Remember it is your money and your home. In years to come, no one will recall the architect responsible for any ghastly mistake, only the person mentioned on the deeds - you!

Where timber-framed buildings have been 'over-extended' in the 20th and 21st centuries, it is sometimes difficult to work out the original plan or shape of the house.

A splendidly spacious new kitchen usually forms part of the smart new extension. The kitchen in particular is always considered the 'heart of the home'. It is warm and cosy and if purpose built and large enough, usually contains a dining table, a comfy chair or two, a TV and a range cooker with the obligatory Labrador squashed up against it, immovable.

The attractive, ancient cottage with the new extension has just undergone 'heart by-pass surgery', so it really is no surprise the older part of the building can often begin to feel cold and unloved. The occupants of an over-extended ancient cottage can sometimes find themselves spending the majority of their time in the newer, often warmer part of the house, reserving use of the older 'wing' for visitors and Christmas. Even heating of the older part of a house can become a secondary consideration, leaving these rooms cold, musty and damp, with all the ambiance of an outside toilet. It is not surprising most of the family prefer to live in the new extension.

So what exactly am I trying to say?

Well, don't rush into doing anything, apart from basic maintenance, for at least the first year or two of ownership. Live in the property and experience how the rooms are used. Consider how an addition would affect the way you live in the existing house. How you could best add an extension (if really necessary) without destroying the character of the ancient building you first fell in love with.

Would a large extension leave the rest of the building neglected?

Could any addition be incorporated in such a way one would regularly have to walk through the old part of the house to access it? Even unused rooms that are frequently walked through feel warmer and more welcoming than those which are constantly closed off.

Do you need more space? Is this really the house for you? Are you just extending to reflect your financial status or to stamp your personality and creativity upon the building? Many owners increase the size of their property when they really have no need for more room. They sometimes struggle to maintain/repair and heat the extra space, but still they keep on extending. Madness!

Where you really are determined to increase the size of your property there are three major points to consider.

The first is, could an addition be accommodated without destruction of original fabric in the existing building? Perhaps an entrance to the new part could lead through an existing doorway. Cutting out stud work should always be a very last option, if at all.

Understanding your frame, the original plan form of your house, will help prevent mistakes

being made, such as the cutting out of original mullion windows or features which you may not recognise until much later.

Secondly, how will the new addition be attached to the older timber-framed building? Any extension adjoined too rigidly and inflexibly to an old timber-framed building risks movement and therefore cracking between the two structures.

Thirdly, what materials will the newer addition be constructed from? **Figure 52**.

In my opinion and experience, any additions to a timber-framed building should only ever be of timber-framed construction. **Figure 53**.

And by timber-framed, I do not mean the wholly inadequate softwood partitioning, nailed together to form the walls of some modern buildings today.

Figure 52 *Traditional materials used in new build blend well with an older structure.*

Figure 53 *A green oak extension to a 16th century house.*

I do mean green oak held together with oak pegs, not a metal bracket or nail in sight. **Figure 54**. In other words, exactly the same methods of construction used to build the ancient timber-framed buildings we admire today.

Figure 54 *A delightful green oak building erected 2003 and built by pupils, staff and parents at a preparatory school in Berkshire. (Visits by prior arrangement contact: Lynne Simmons tel: 01344 467200)*

A timber-framed structure, whether brand new or five hundred years old, has a certain amount of flexibility, so anything you attach to it should also be able to accommodate slight movement. This is something brick, breeze-block, gypsum plaster and cement cannot do without showing signs of stress.

Apart from this, many new extensions built today are required to have extremely deep footings, up to three meters in some cases. Whereas ancient timber-framed buildings, as already mentioned, were originally built on a very shallow brick/flint rubble or stone plinth, sometimes of only a few inches in depth. So, one can imagine the damage digging excessively deep footings might cause next to an existing ancient structure.

Where new additions are concerned, unlike rigid breeze-block or brick built extensions, a timber-framed structure is best erected on shallow footings as the load is evenly spread over the whole timber sole plate running around the base of the walls. This method of construction is far less disruptive to the foundation of an existing timber-framed building, not to mention a good deal less costly to you, the home owner. A green oak timber-framed extension can also be attached to the older building using the minimum of fixings. This allows the newer structure to move and settle within its first few years without disturbing the old and is vitally important where moisture rich green oak is concerned.

Old reclaimed oak should never be used for any new addition to an original timber-framed building for all of the reasons mentioned in an earlier section. **See section 6** (page 37). The Timber Frame.

If you decide to build an extension using green oak, the same principles of care and repair used throughout your ancient building apply. All external 'protection' layers such as render, weather board or paint, should all be of the 'breathing' variety.

Ground level flooring within a new extension, due to current building regulations, may have to be laid on a damp proof membrane, although totally unnecessary in my opinion. However, provided the membrane does not stop internally at the base of the walls of the new extension but travels on through to the outside, in other words, is continuous, this should not cause problems for the newer structure in the future.

However, one should bear in mind the new extension damp proof membrane could have the potential to encourage ground moisture (unable to escape through the new non-breathing floor) towards the older building. If the older building has 'breathing' flooring throughout, this should not cause a problem. Where solid, impermeable floors exist in the older structure, perhaps the other side of a party wall in certain cases, owners could discover moisture and fungal growth appearing at the base of this. The party wall may begin to act like a sponge, the only route for trapped moisture to escape.

Excessive moisture can speed up decay of the fabric of the wall, whether brick or daub, breaking it down, possibly even causing movement where conditions are favourable.
At the very least fungal growth could become a continual annoyance, impossible to eradicate permanently unless impervious flooring in the older part of the house is carefully removed and replaced with a 'breathing' floor. ie: natural materials, unsealed, laid directly upon the earth, on a base of sand or chalk.

Therefore, if you are currently viewing a timber-framed building which has had recent additions, it would be prudent to enquire when these were built. If they are very new, problems may not arise for several years. You might also enquire what materials were used in their construction and, where a building is Listed, whether any newer (late 20th or early 21st century) additions received the necessary Listed Building Consent.

This last point is of vital importance because if Listed Building Consent was not obtained, a new and completely innocent owner could be required to restore a building back to its former unextended state prior to any unauthorised works.

Check the plan of the building with your solicitor and make certain you are not caught out by someone else's past misdemeanors.

17. Listed Buildings - Your Local Authority

If you are considering buying or working on an historic building (timber-framed or otherwise) it is likely to be Listed by English Heritage as 'being of architectural or historic interest'.

This means much of what you might intend to change, alter or repair, whether using traditional methods and products or not, may require Listed Building Consent, or at the very least close consultation with your local authority conservation department/officer.

Although officers within each local authority may work with the same set of Government guidelines when advising homeowners in matters of repair, care and alteration, each individual officer may have their own opinion on what exactly constitutes repair, general maintenance or significant alteration.

One local authority conservation officer may consider completely replacing a sole plate around the base of a house no more than a repair, not requiring Listed Building Consent. Another may consider this a significant alteration not only requiring a Listed Building Application but also submission of detailed plans showing exactly how the work will be undertaken or perhaps even what mix will be used in the lime mortar, plaster or daub.

From the very beginning, before work starts, you will need to consult your local authority conservation department (or planning department in some areas) to seek advice in this regard.

When you do, it is worth bearing in mind local authority officers employed to work with owners of historic buildings are not there to frustrate, annoy or prevent you from doing anything at all to your home.

They are there to guide, advise and assist you. To help you look after an asset to their area. Always remember, you both have the same goals. You both care about the same building. It is in your interest to work together and to consider the opinions of someone employed to help you make sometimes difficult decisions.

It may be your home for a short while, but you are looking after the nations heritage. It is a difficult job to do alone, so readily accept help and advice from someone who may have more experience than you and you will get along just fine.

Of course, there are historically important buildings around today which escaped the 1970's Listing but are still worthy of the same TLC and consideration afforded to a Listed building. Whether your timber-framed building is Listed or not, seek advice and think very carefully before you destroy any part of it.

18. Adjoining buildings - Semi-detached, terraced and town

If you are considering buying a semi-detached or terraced timber-framed building that was originally part of (adjoined to) the building next door (i.e.: the centre section of a former open hall house), you might wish to consider the structural condition of your neighbours property.

Because of the very nature of their construction, being made up from dozens of separate parts, timber-framed buildings are often subject to brutal and on occasion structurally challenging alteration, much of this carried out by those ignorant of the important function of the timber(s) they are removing. **See section 8** (pages 39-42). What parts of the frame are missing?

Collars, tie-beams, braces, wall plates and even crown posts are often cut out without a minutes consideration for the consequences.

In extreme cases, the cutting through of an inconveniently situated timber, such as a roof collar or tie beam in the property next door, could lead to structural movement of one or more of the adjoining timber-framed properties.

Although it is a criminal offence to remove any timbers within a Listed building without the necessary consent, many timber-framed buildings are not Listed and sadly even those that are still suffer from much illegal alteration behind closed doors. Buildings situated in popular (sought after) towns and villages, where properties regularly change hands or may provide retail facilities, are particularly vulnerable and can be subject to constant alteration by each new owner.

Even if the adjoining property is in immaculate condition today, who knows what chain saw wielding mad person will move in tomorrow?

And don't forget, should the adjoining neighbours choose to insert a damp proof membrane or plaster and paint the party wall using impermeable products, this could encourage moisture towards your part of the building causing problems for you both.

If your town or village property happens to abut pavements or roads laid with impermeable materials such as bitumen or concrete, this could also encourage moisture towards the walls of your building. This problem is not specific to timber-framed buildings as any walk around an historic town will reveal. Many period buildings, including Georgian and Victorian, which have impermeable surfaces laid immediately up to their external walls not only show signs of mould growth and trapped moisture but, in some cases, the dreaded drill holes left by a damp proof company. **See figure 39** (page 48).

Home owners unaware why moisture is becoming trapped at the base of their walls call out their friendly 'damp proof chap'. He usually diagnoses rising damp, suggesting the affected walls are injected with a 'magic potion' which will miraculously vanish away all damp problems, at least until their guarantee has run out, the company has gone bust or you have moved.

As discussed in section 2 (page 24). concerning paths surrounding a timber-framed building, all that is usually required is a means of escape (both internally and externally) for trapped moisture. A breathing gap between path/road and property wall will, in most cases considerably relieve the situation where trapped ground moisture is a problem.

When one considers many of the road and pathway surfaces directly situated outside our homes were of the permeable type (i.e. earth, stones or grass) until around the 1950's, it is not surprising many period buildings are beginning to suffer today, after nearly a generation of incarceration.

Buildings need people

Many people consider an idyllic, thatched, beamed cottage the ideal country retreat and timber-framed cottages all over the country are frequently snapped up for use as holiday homes.

The truth of the matter is our organic, breeze loving timber-framed building does not make the ideal holiday cottage when infrequently inhabited.

A timber-framed building shut up for weeks at a time, hermetically sealed, unable to 'breathe', can begin to smell like an old pair of socks, due to a build up of moisture inside.

When a timber-framed building is not subject to regular ventilation problems with fungal growth can quickly ensue.

All buildings function better when they are lived in and cared for. Regularly opening windows and doors and lighting fires or candles all help to create an ambiance no once a month weekend visit could ever do.

All organic things thrive in a healthy environment. Your living, breathing, expanding and contracting with the seasons timber-framed home is no different.

Neglected it will deteriorate. Looked after correctly it will last for many hundreds of years more for future generations to admire and enjoy!

To conclude

By now, I hope you will have a much clearer understanding of how to live in harmony within your timber-framed home.

The rules for success are as simple as the methods and materials used in its construction.

Much of the deterioration we witness today has occurred within the last century and is predominantly due to well meaning, but misguided renovation and repair techniques which sadly still go on today.

We are fortunate in that there is still time to halt the decay, to preserve what we have left and to learn so much from the care and repair of these beautiful buildings.

If you are just at the beginning of your timber-framed journey, take your time. Consider carefully everything you do. Never repair anything until you have a clear understanding of why it failed in the first place and, whenever possible, concentrate on one job at a time.

Attend as many courses in traditional building skills as you can. Begin by learning everything you need to know to help you understand your building better.

Talk to other timber-framed homeowners to obtain unbiased, impartial advice together with invaluable moral support.

Looking after a timber-framed building can sometimes feel like a huge responsibility, but I have never encountered anything more rewarding and enjoyable. I hope you feel the same.

In this house we reside,
Full of wonder, full of pride,
Those who built it must have been
men with courage, strength, a
dream.

Blood and sweat, tears and toil,
Rising upwards from the soil,
Planted firmly, as we see,
Here, for all eternity.

PBH

References and Bibliography

Rideout, Brian (2000) Timber Decay in Buildings, English Heritage, The Buildings and Monuments Commission for England, and Historic Scotland, an Executive Agency of the Scottish Executive. ISBN 0-419-18820-7

Cathedral Communications Ltd   (2001) The Building Conservation Directory. A guide to specialist suppliers, consultants and craftsmen in traditional building conservation, refurbishment and design. ISBN 190091517-0 Pages 51 - 52 & 79 -81

Sandon, Eric F.R.I.B.A., F.S.A. (1977) Suffolk Houses, A Study of Domestic Architecture. Baron Publishing Ltd. ISBN 0 90202868 5

Cunnington, Pamela (1980) How Old Is Your House? Alphabooks Ltd. An imprint of A & C Black (Publishers) Ltd. ISBN 0-7136-3022-1

Harris, Richard (1978) Discovering Timber-Framed Buildings. Shire Publications Ltd. ISBN 0-7478-0215-7

Schofield, Jane (1995) Lime In Building. Black Dog Press. ISBN 0 9524341 1 3

Twinch, Carol. (2001) Tithe War 1918-1939. The Countryside In Revolt. Media Associates. ISBN 0 9521499 2 3

The Building Limes Forum (2003) Vol. 10. The Journal of the Building Limes Forum to encourage expertise and understanding in the use of building limes. ISSN 1479 6902. Pages 48-52.